the ABCs of SLO County

Written by Jennifer Kirn
Paintings by Kathleen Crawford

First edition, August 2023
Copyright © 2023 Jennifer Kirn

ISBN: 978-1-939502-55-1

Published by Penciled In
5319 Barrenda Avenue
Atascadero, CA 93422
penciledin.com

Paintings by
    Kathleen Crawford
Book and Cover Layout by
    Benjamin Daniel Lawless

No part of this book may be reproduced or transmitted in any part or form by any means including but not limited to digital, electronic, analog, photocopying, recording, or storage retrieval systems without permission from the author, except a reviewer who may quote a single brief passage or use on illustration in a review. The inclusion of any location, event, or service in this book should not be considered to reflect endorsement, sponsorship, approval or association of or with any individuals or entities that own, operate, or are otherwise associated with those mentioned in this book.

There are many people who have brought this work to fruition and for that I am grateful. First and foremost, the talented, Katie. Without you, this project would not be shared with others. To all the local businesses and people in our county who make SLO, SLO and have granted their permission to be included. To Ben, for enduring round 2.
To my friends and family, thank you for your encouraging words and support and lastly, to Declan, for without your presence and inspiration this would not be possible.

Thank you and all my love!

Jenn

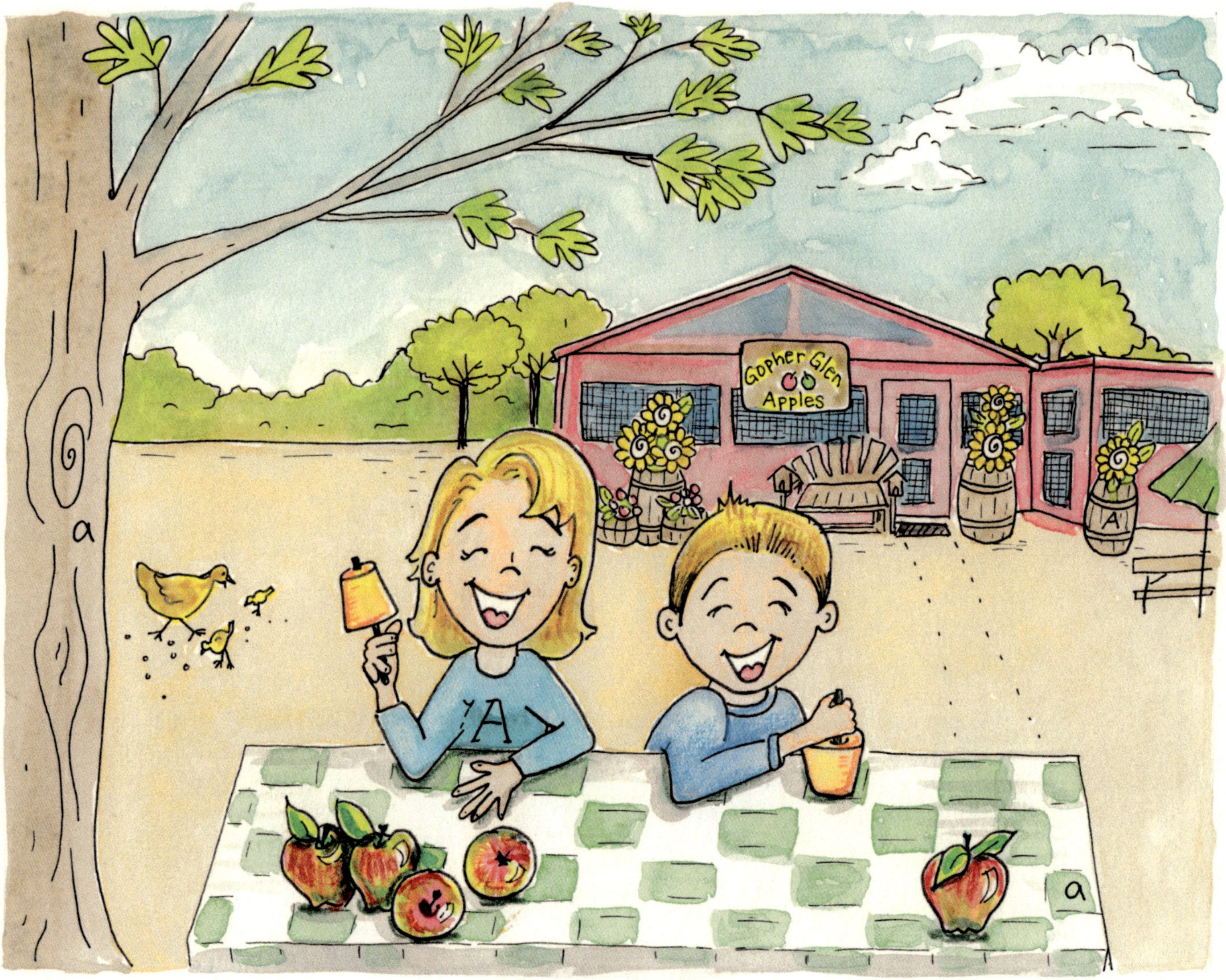
Gopher Glen
Apples
a
A
A
a

A is for the Apples
we eat at Gopher Glen

B is for the Beaches where surfers hang ten

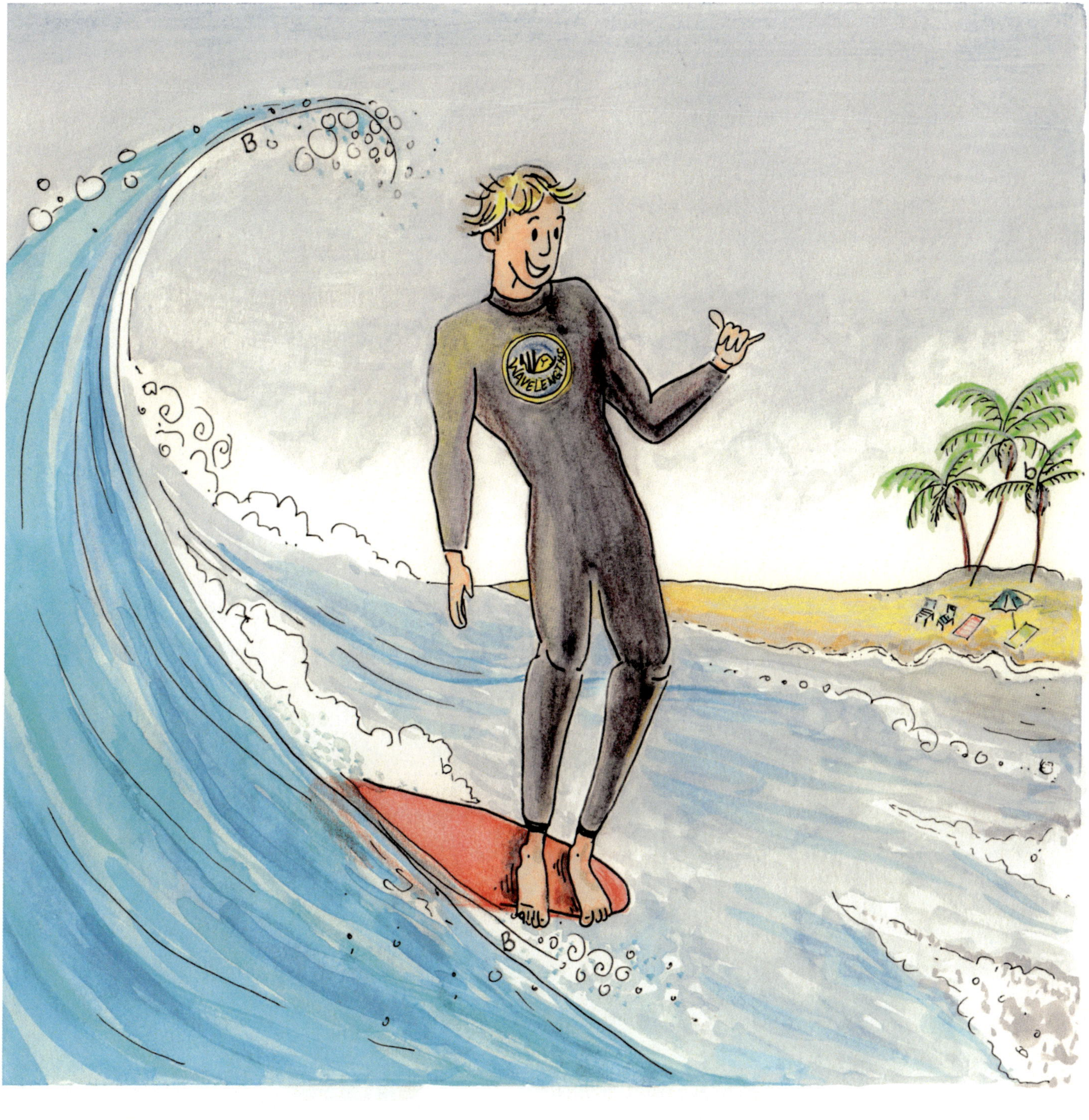
WAVELENGTHS

BROWN BUTTER COOKIE COMPANY
Life's Short EAT COOKIES
Brown Butter Sea Salt
• original
• cocoa
• honey
• espresso
• cinnamon
• cocoa mint

C is for Cayucos and the
brown butter cookies that are round

D is for our Dinosaur Caves where a playground can be found

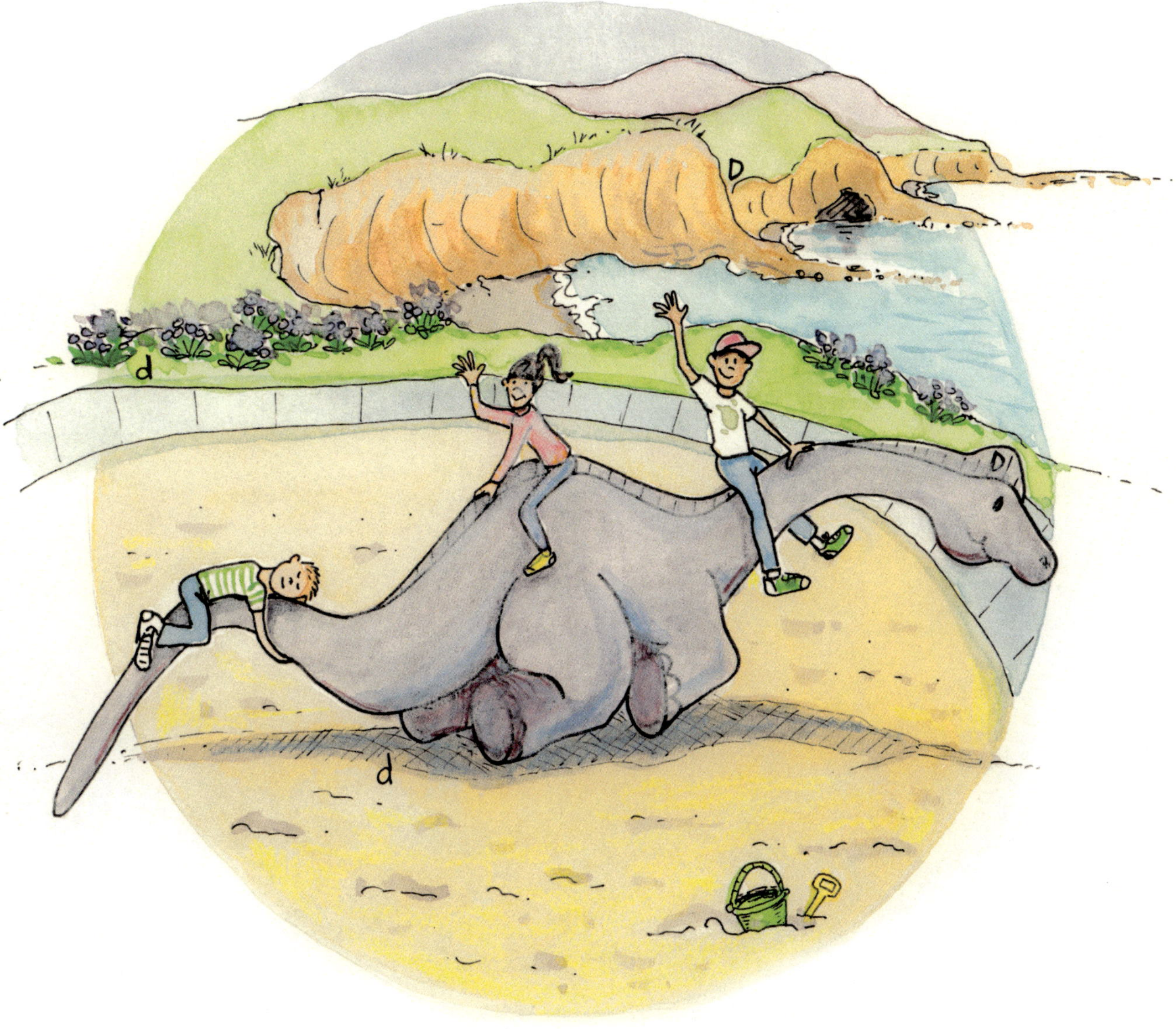
D
d
D
d

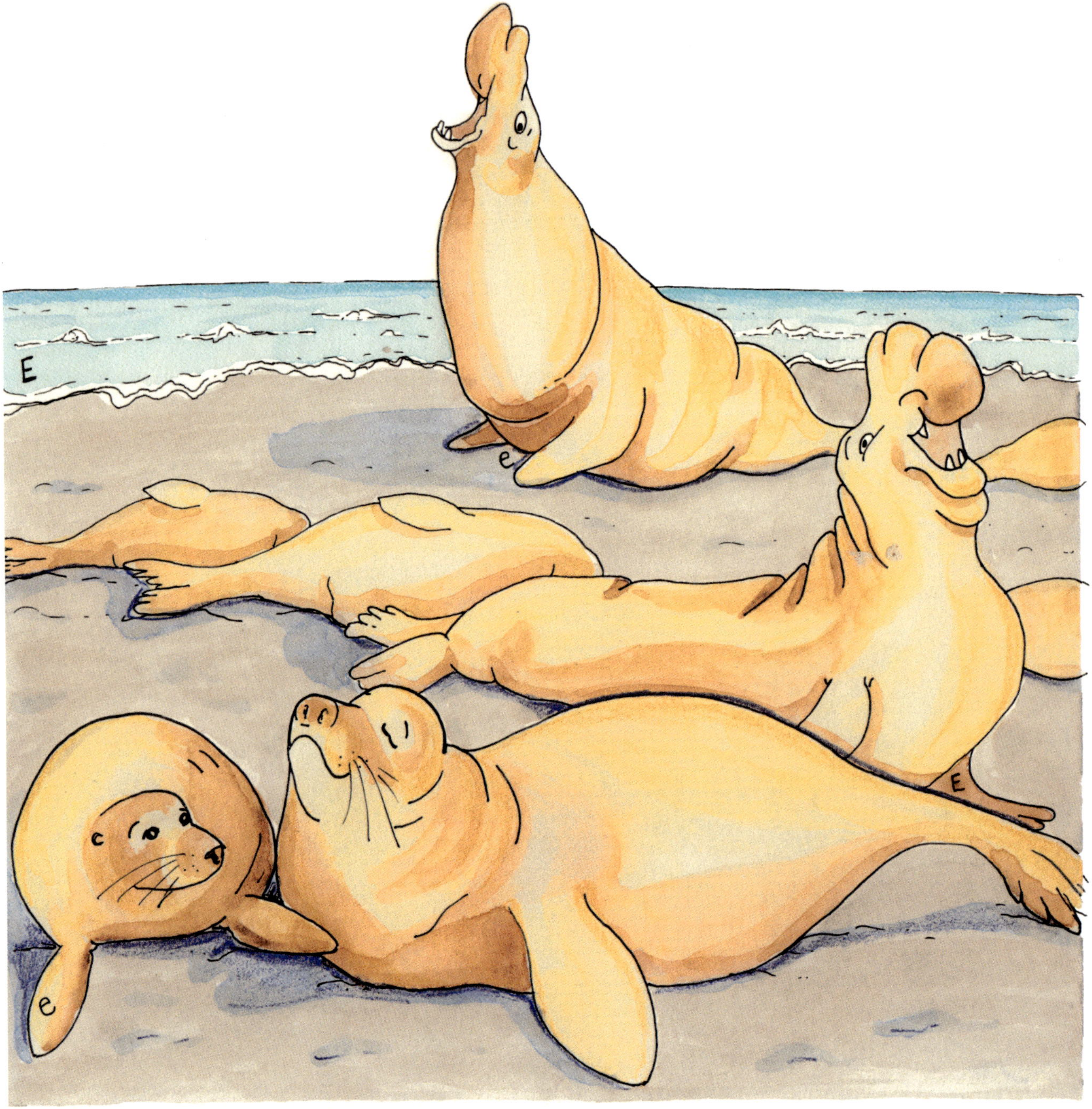
E
e
E
e

E is for the Elephant Seals
who sunbathe on the shore

F is for Fiscalini Ranch
where we like to explore

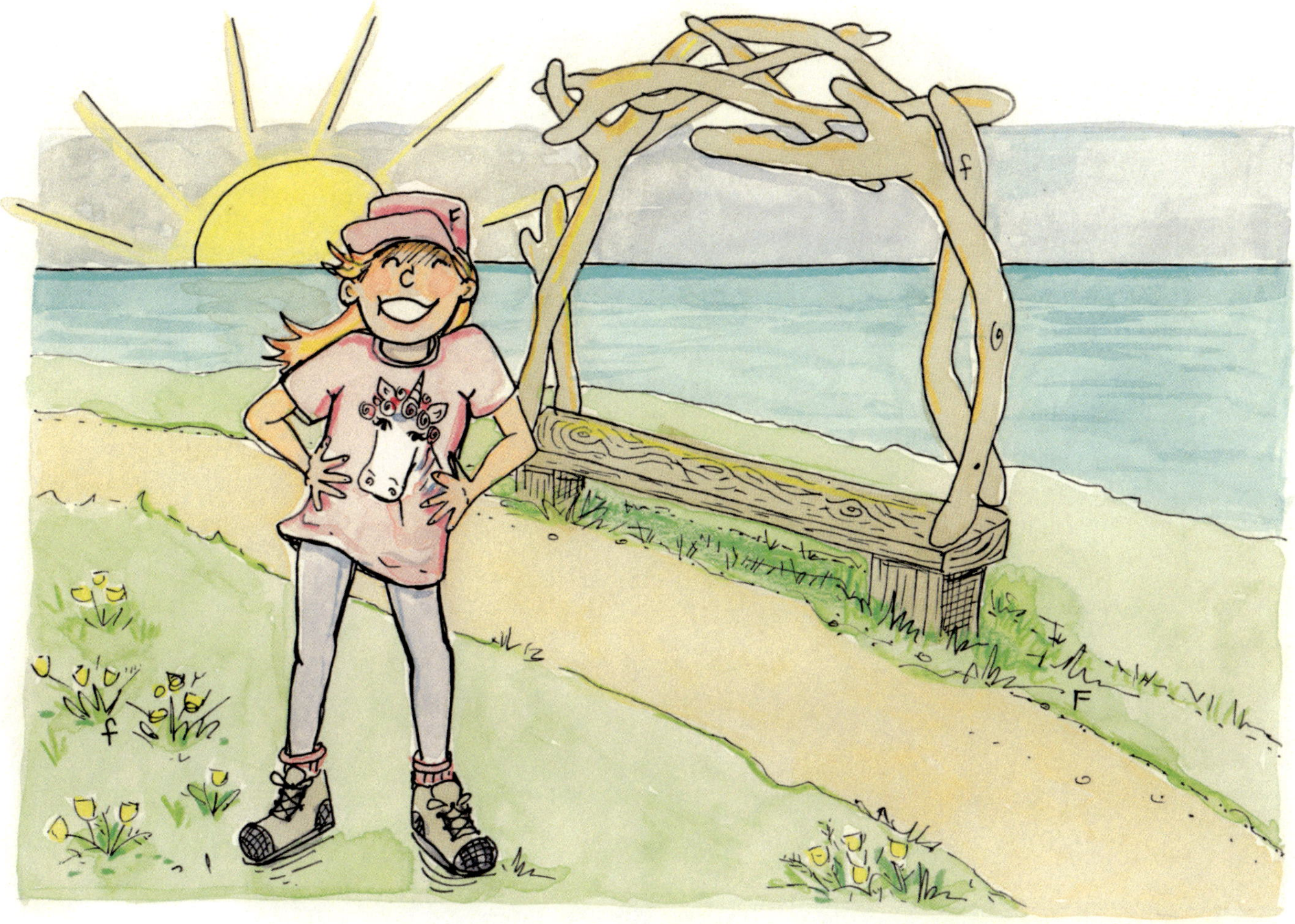

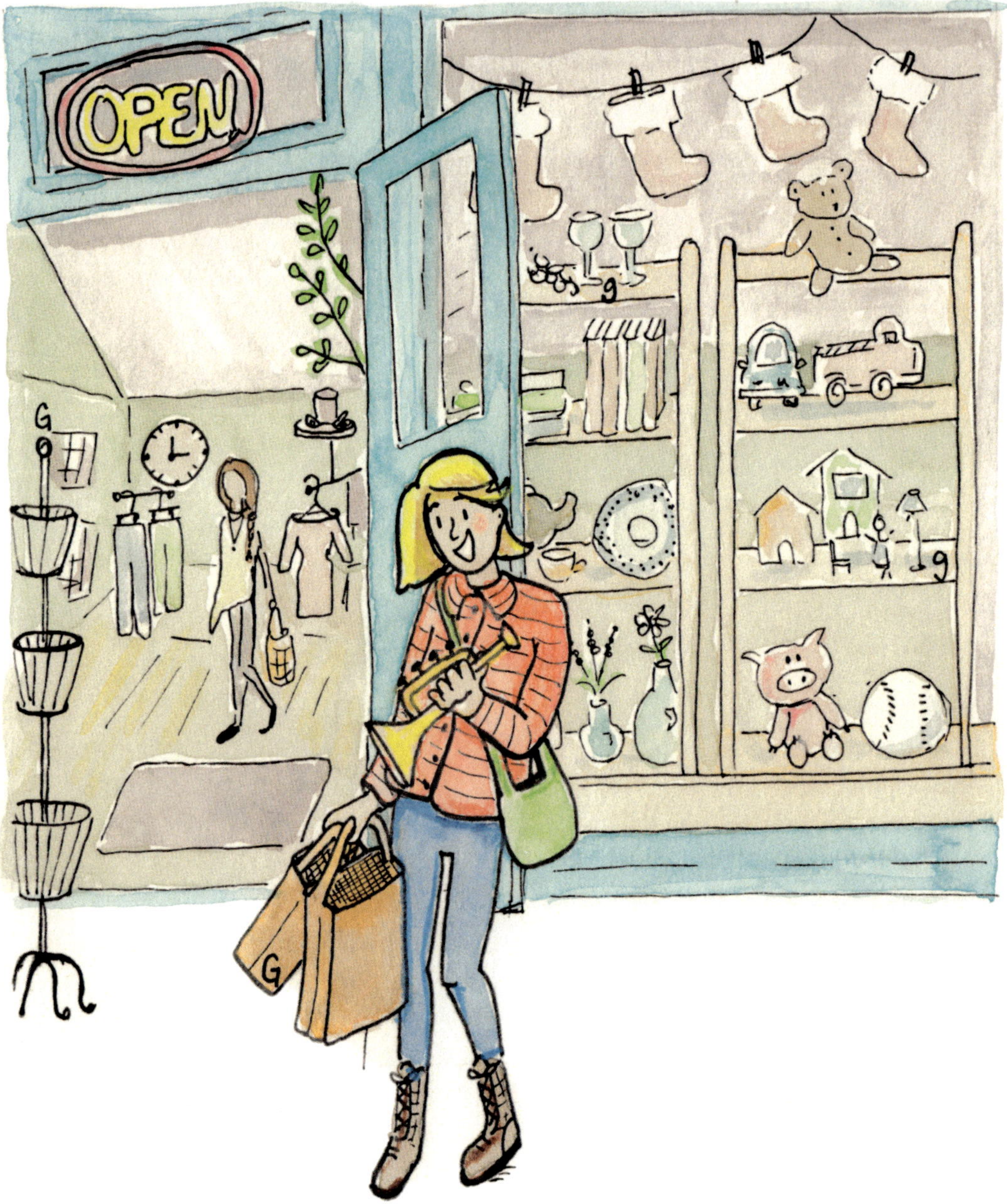
OPEN

G is for Grover Beach
and its fun thrift shops

H is for Hearst Castle where the zebras are worth a stop

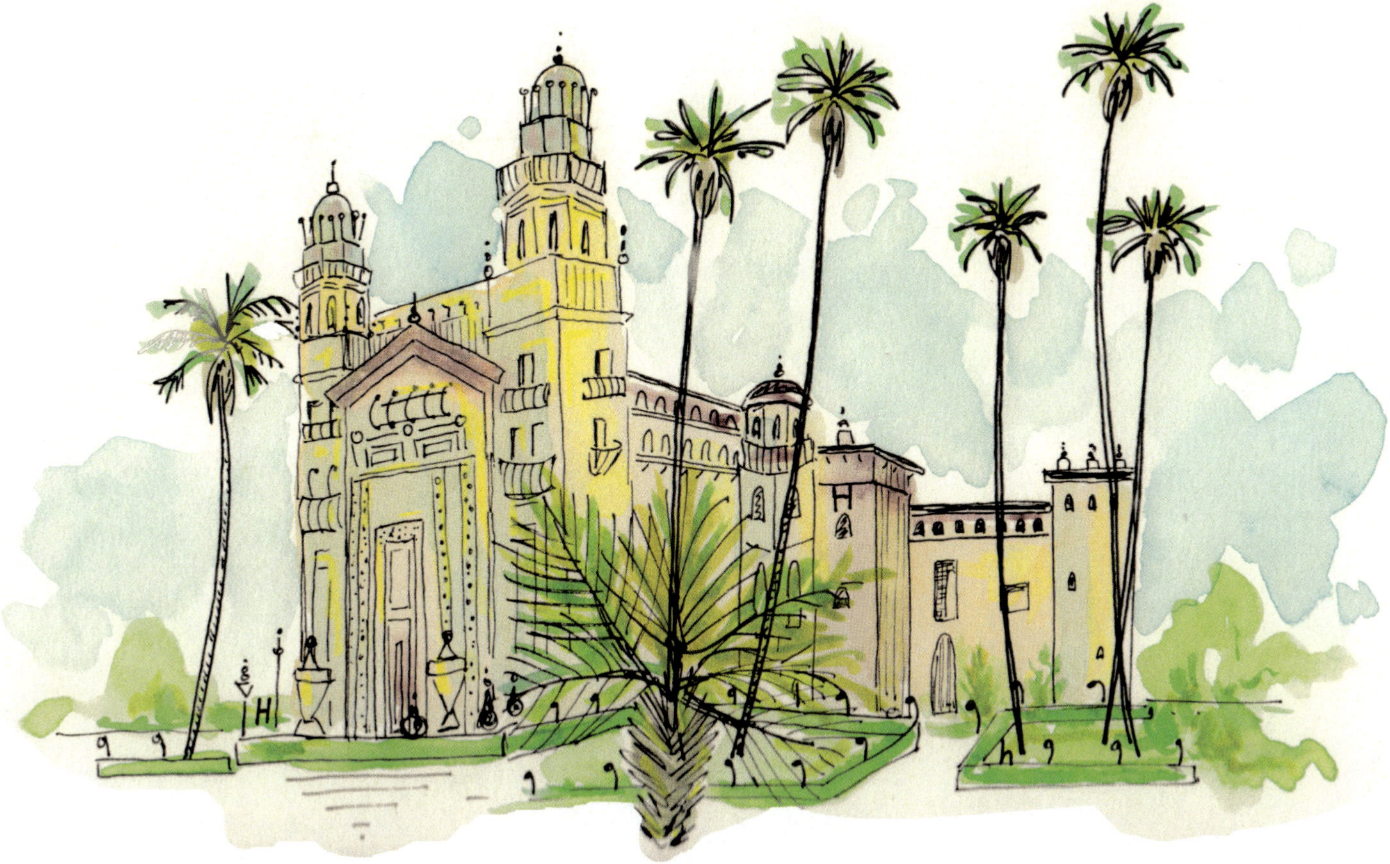

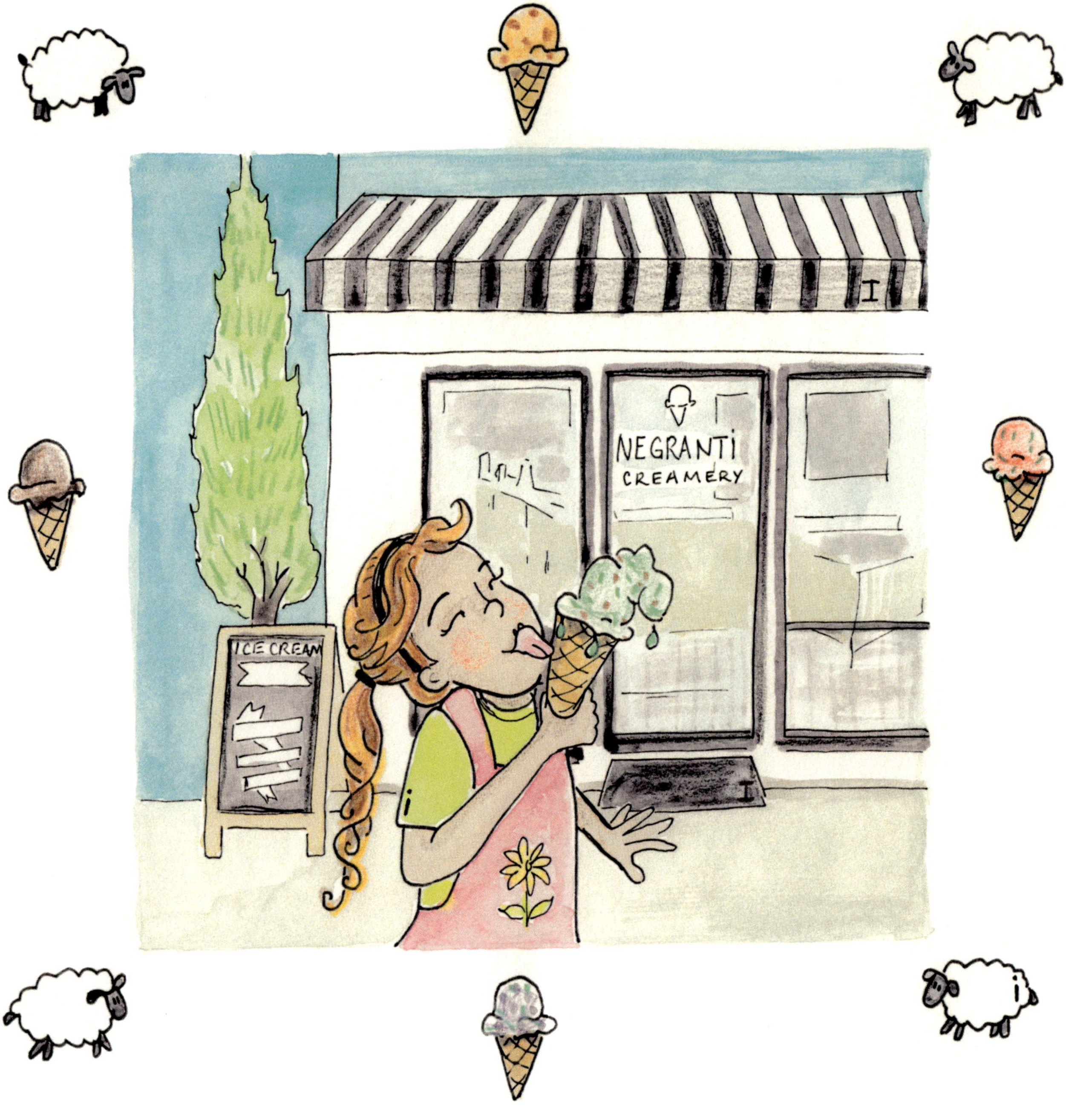
NEGRANTI
CREAMERY
ICE CREAM

I is for the Ice Cream we devour
from Negranti Creamery

J is for Jack Creek Farms with their pumpkins and vibrant fall scenery

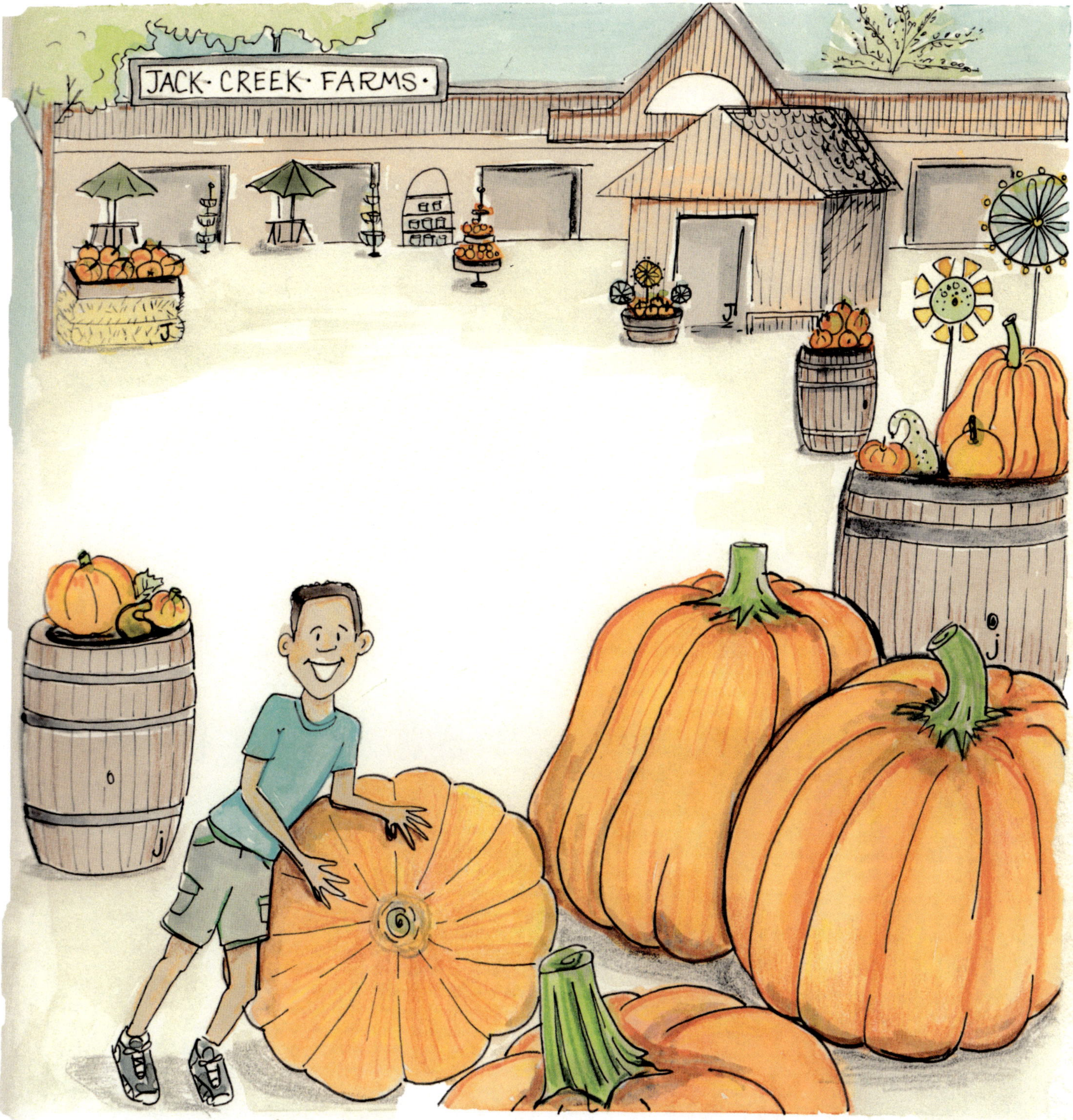
JACK·CREEK·FARMS·

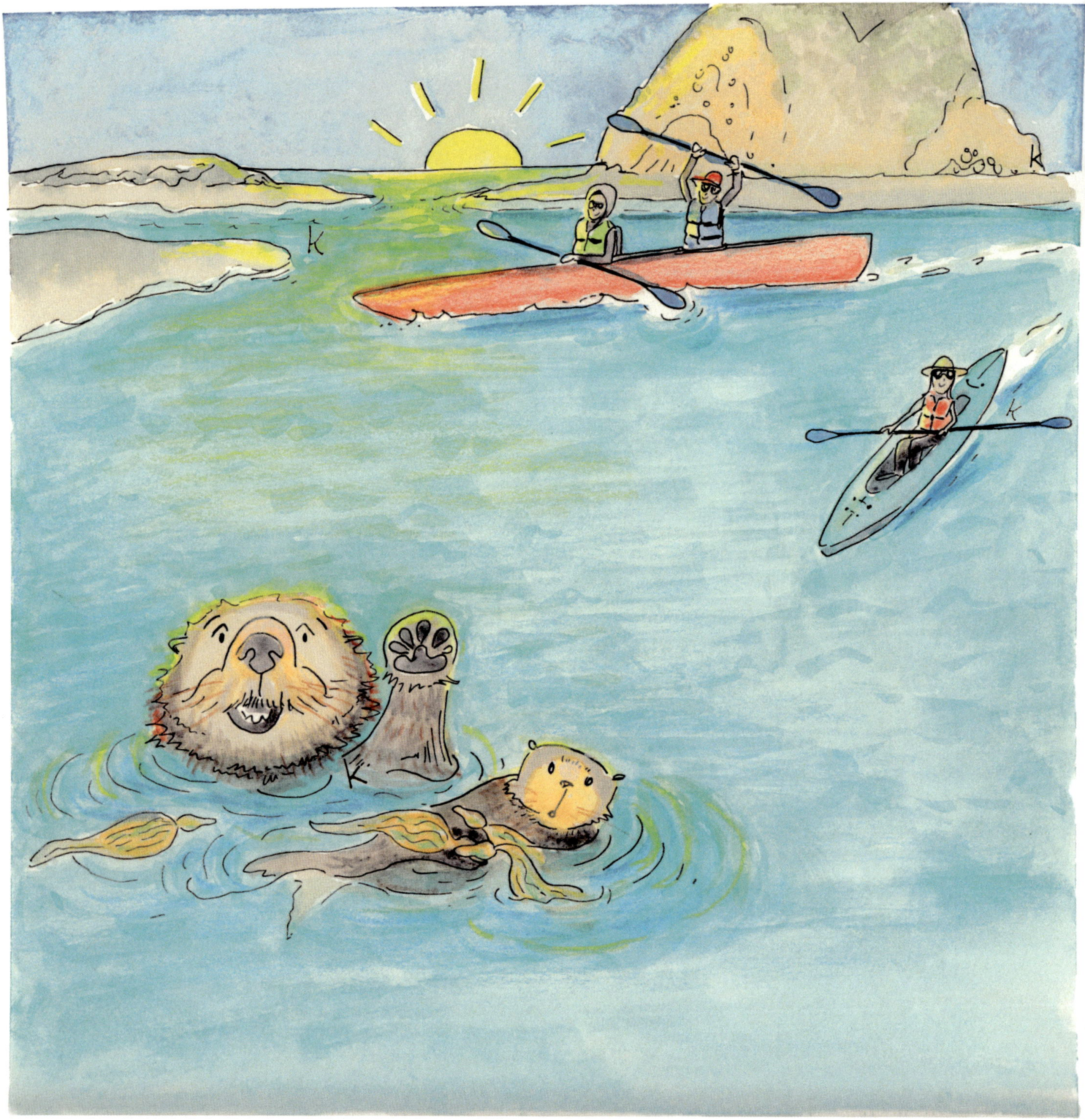

K is for Kayaking where we paddle on the bay

L is for Laguna Lake and the many dogs that play

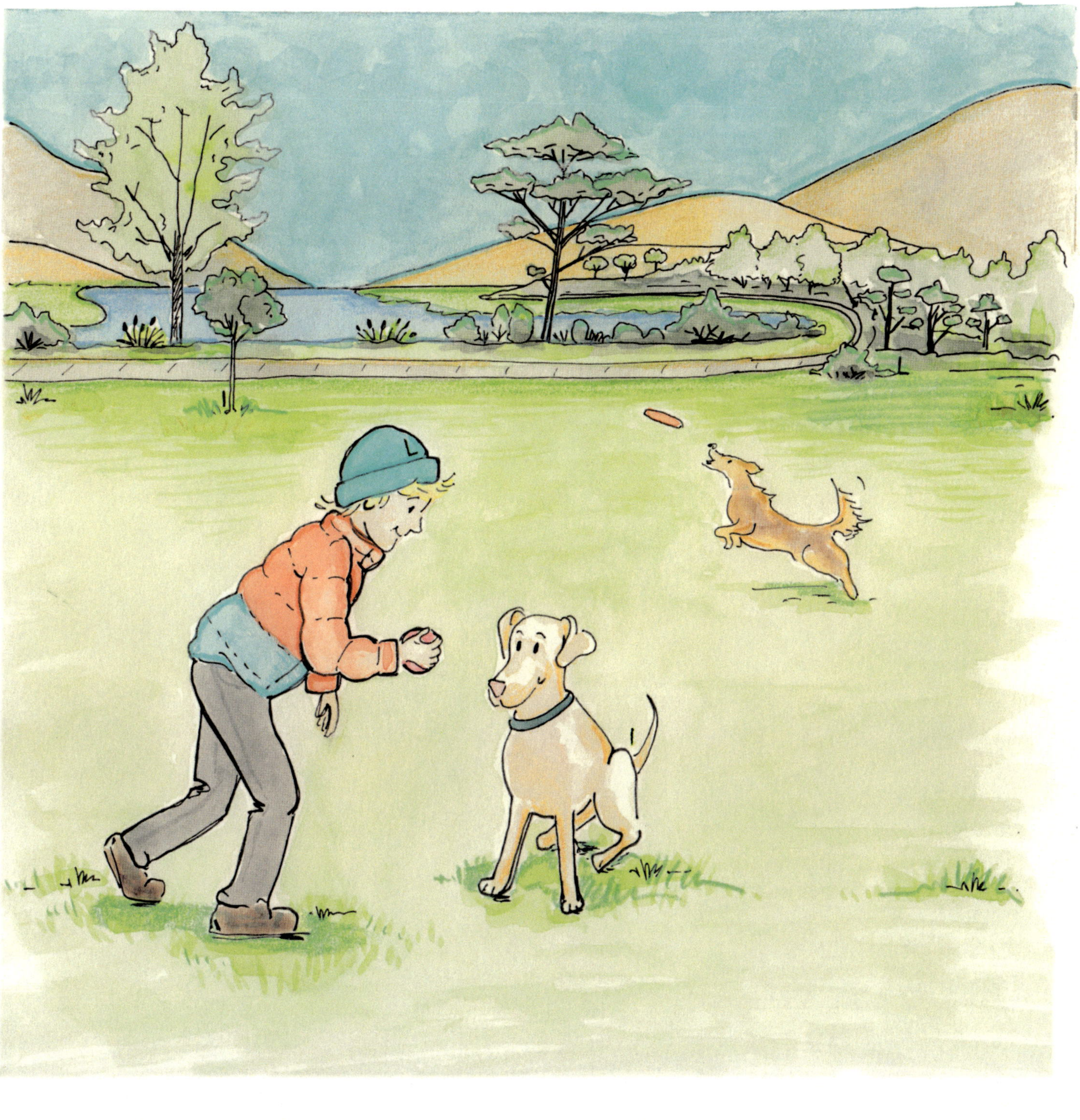

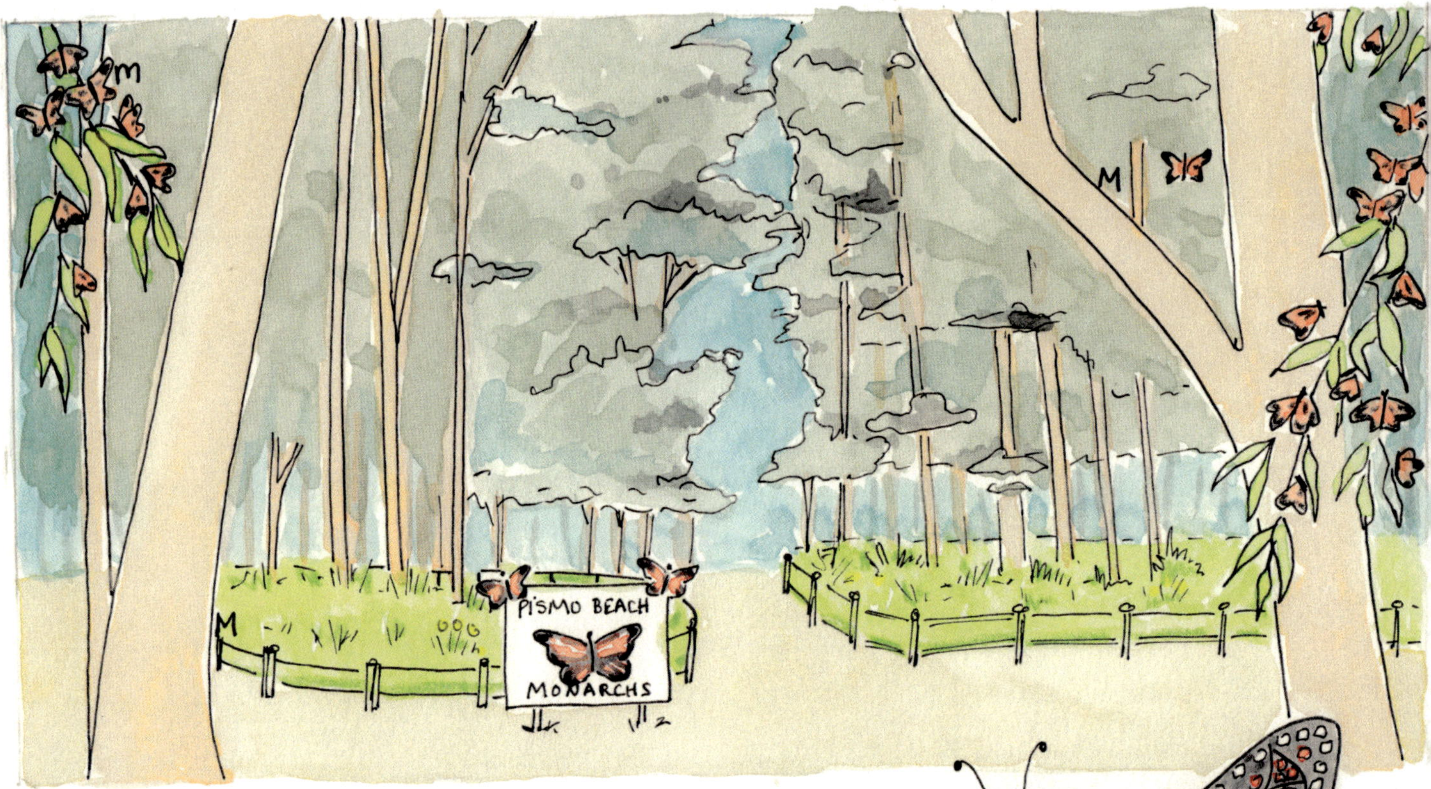
PISMO BEACH
MONARCHS

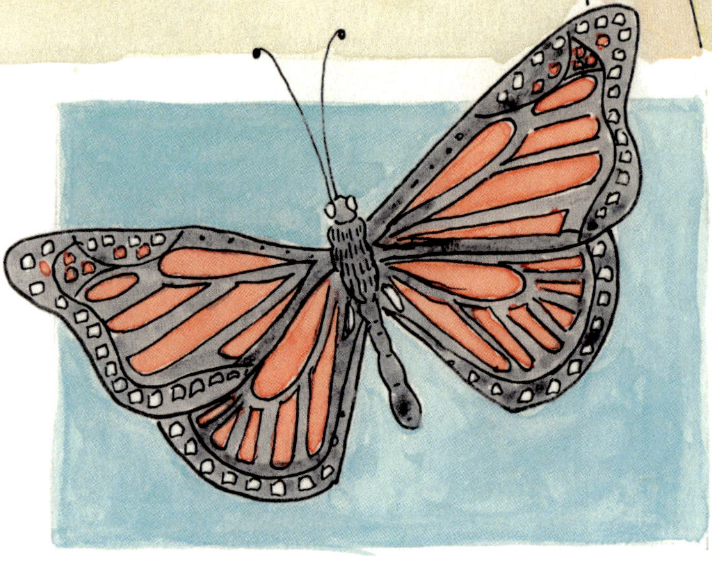

M is for Monarch Grove and all the butterflies in the trees

N is for Nipomo
and the Dana Adobe

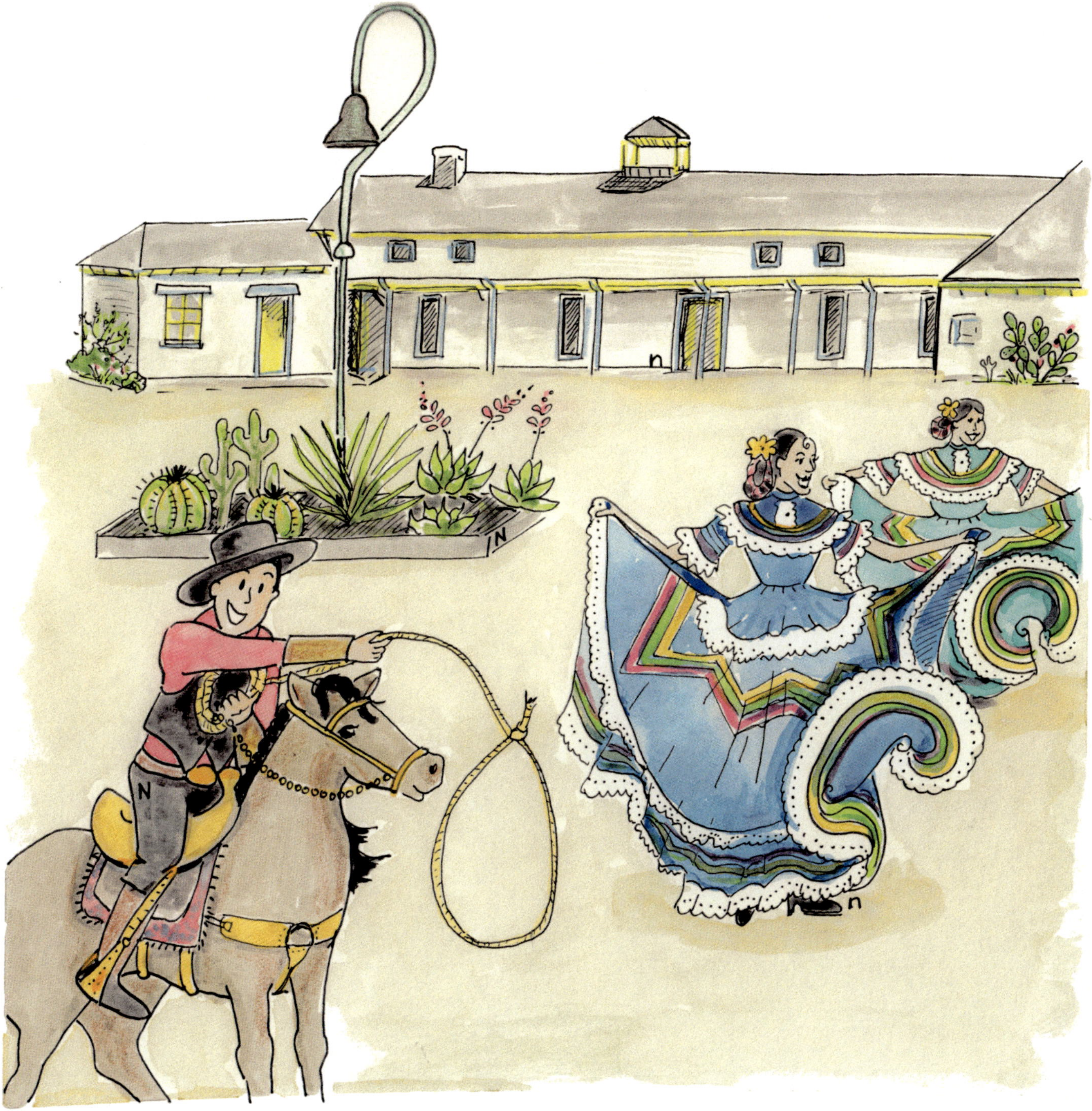

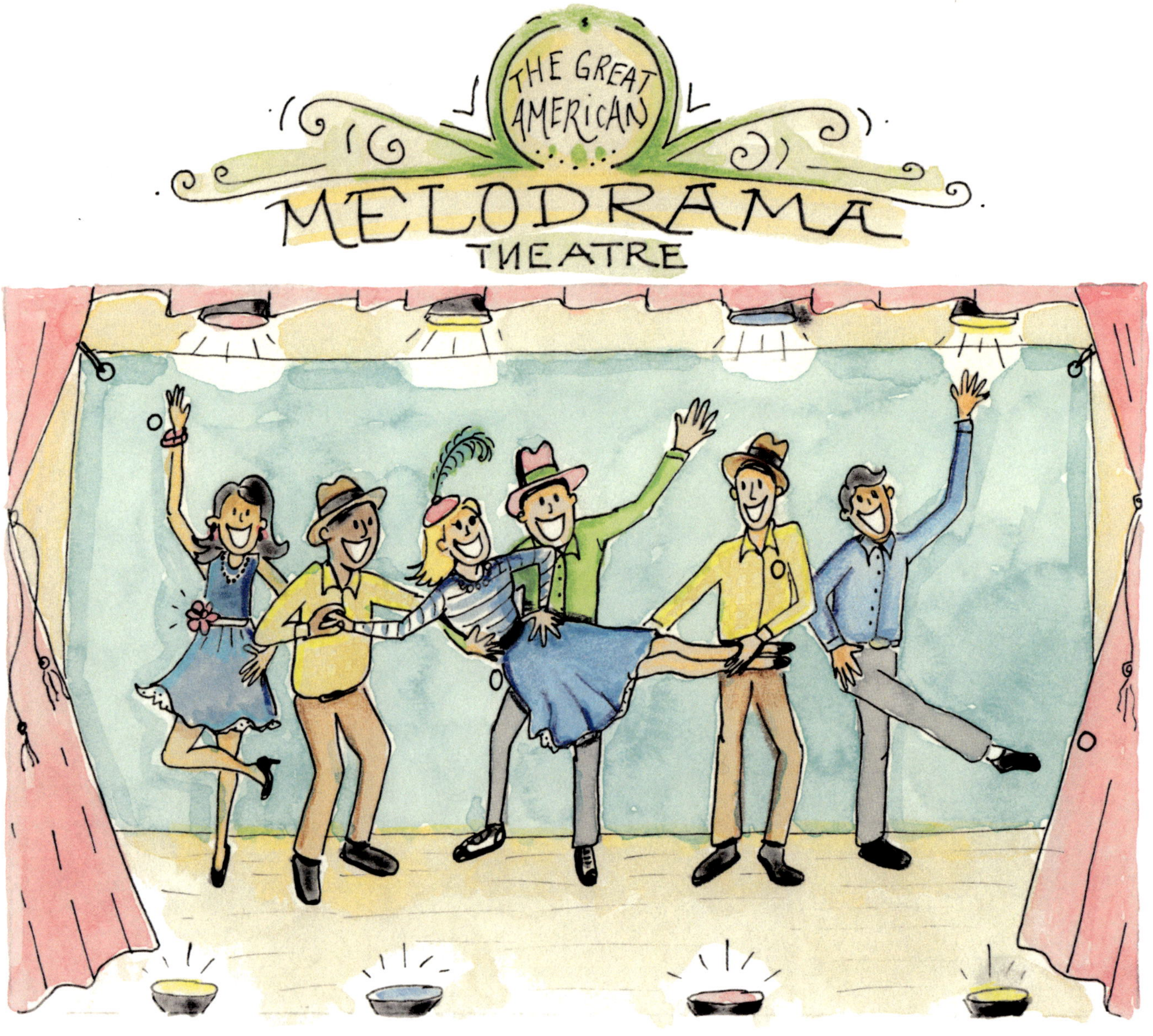
THE GREAT AMERICAN
MELODRAMA
THEATRE

O is for Oceano and the Great American Melodrama

P is for Pismo and the beach strolling llamas

October 1988

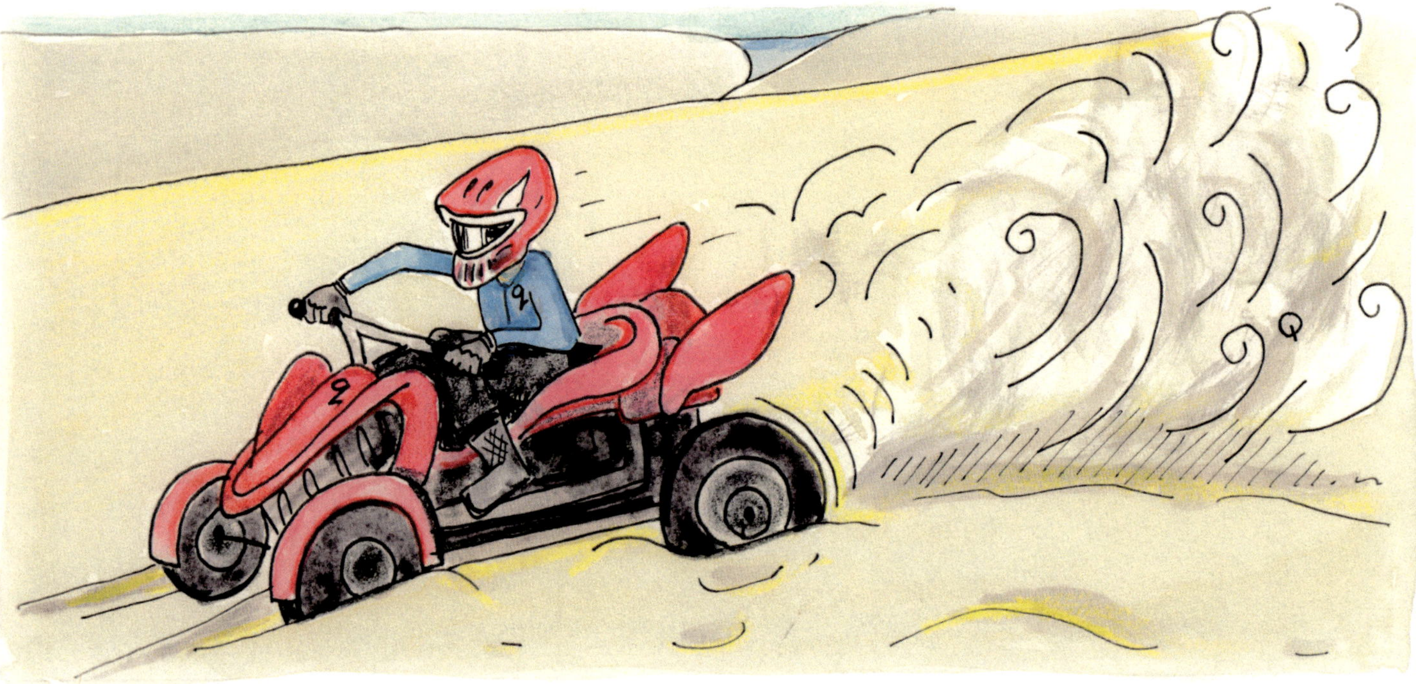

Q is for the Quad bikes that are super fun to ride.

R is for the Railroad Museum
a place of historical pride

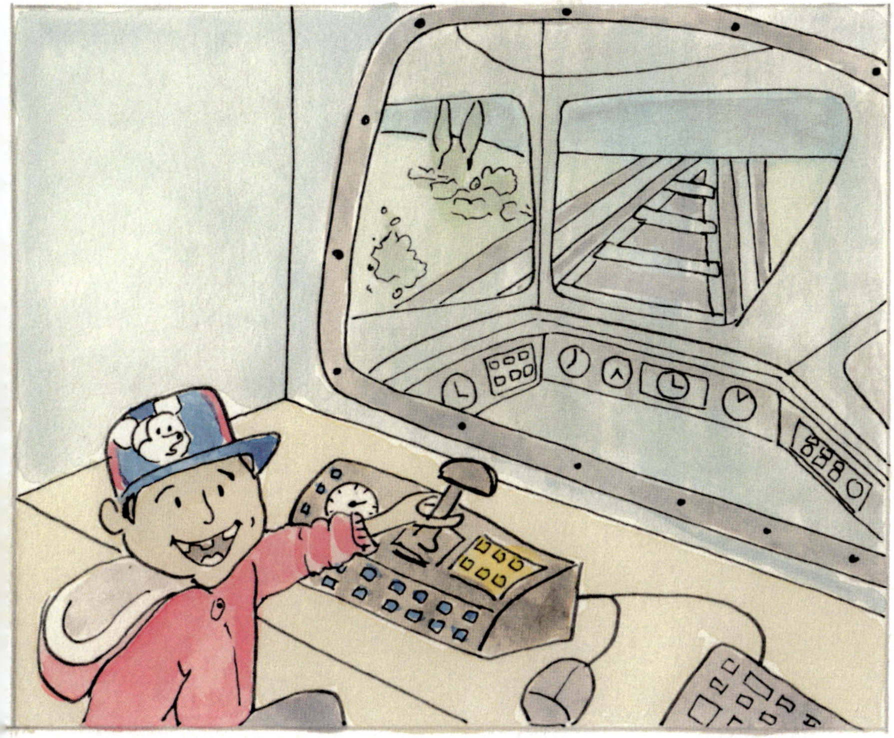

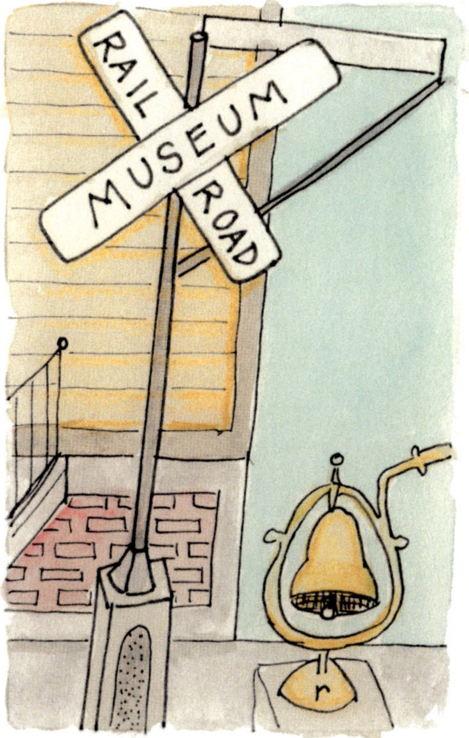
RAIL
MUSEUM
ROAD

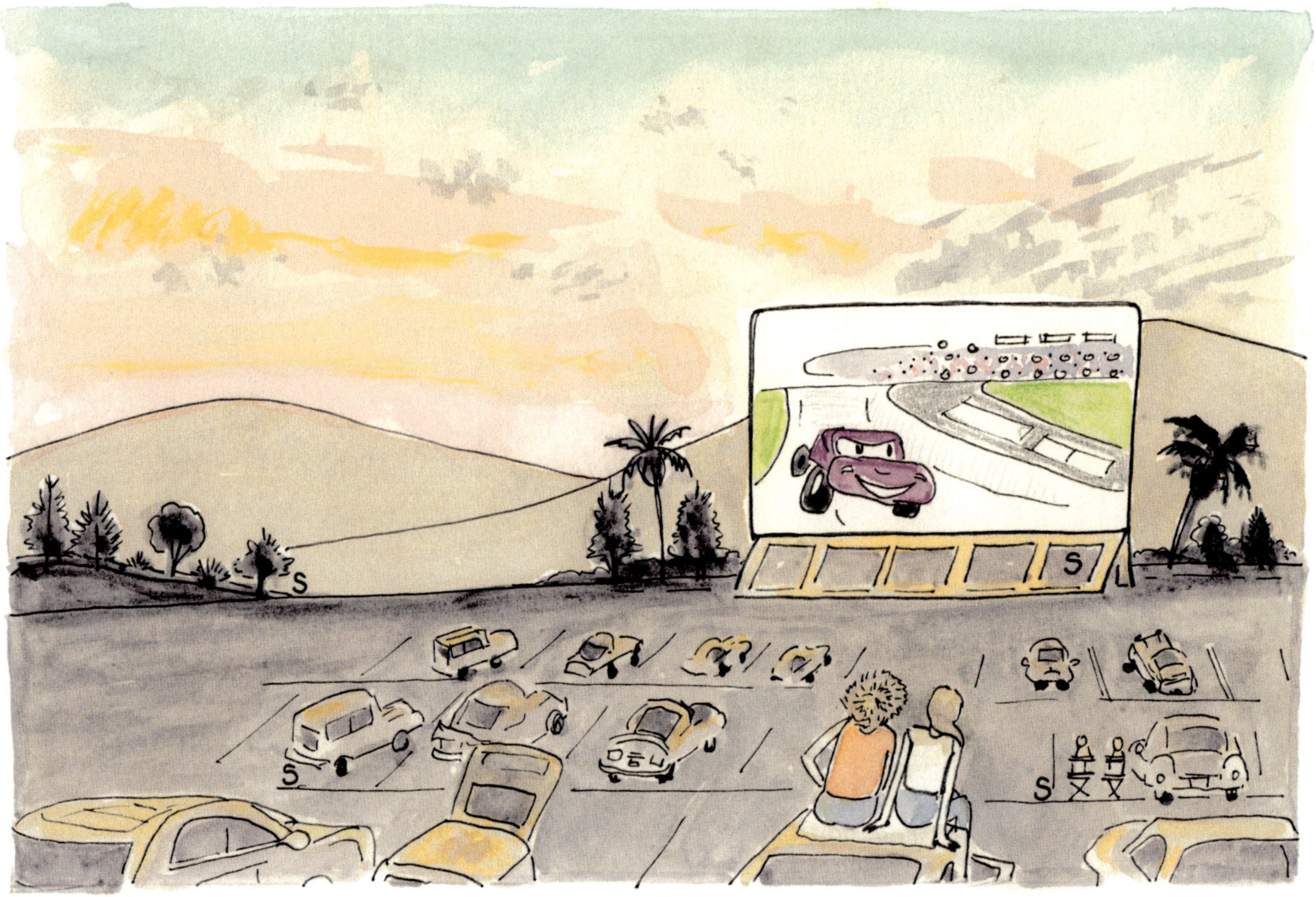

S is for the Sunset Drive-In
that we visit in the dark

T is for the Tide pools at
Montaña De Oro State Park

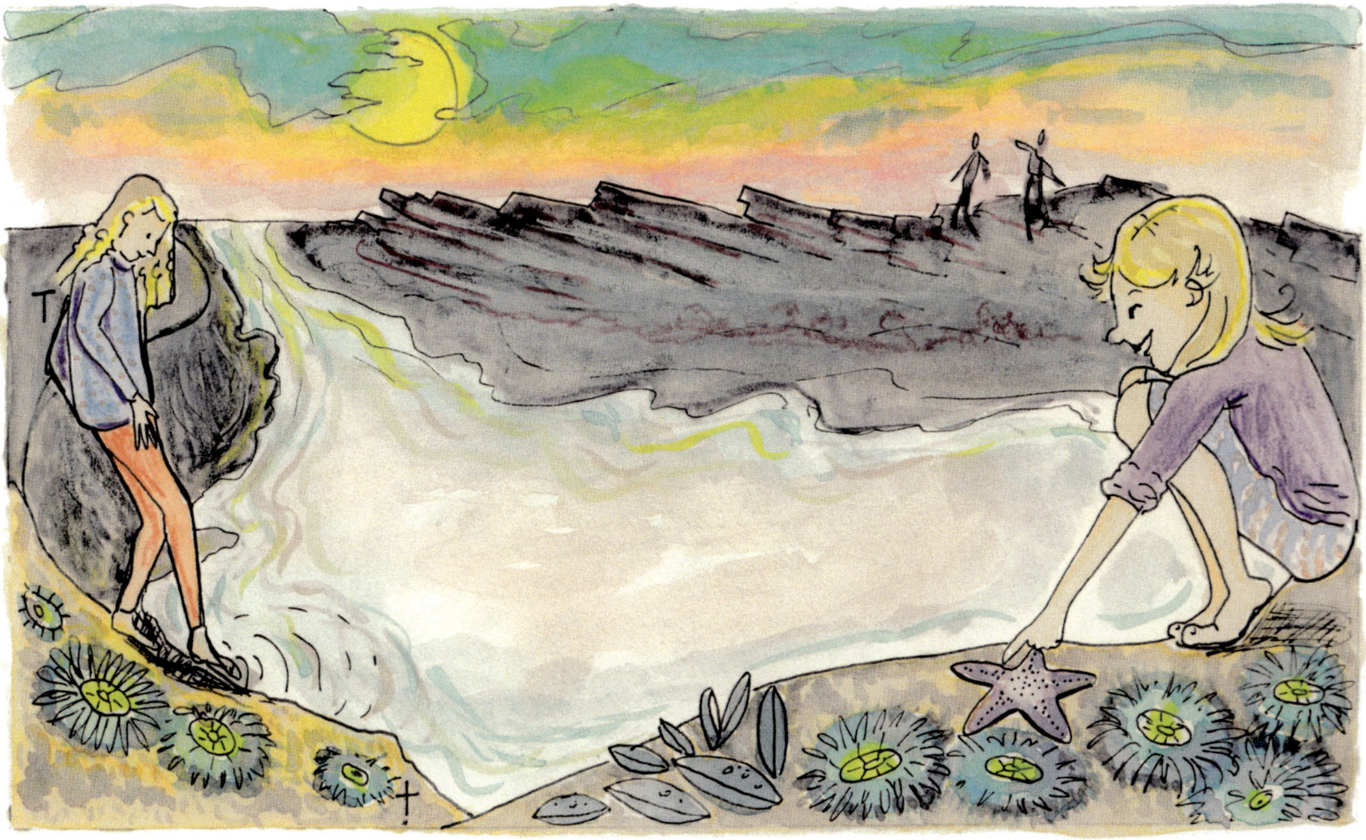

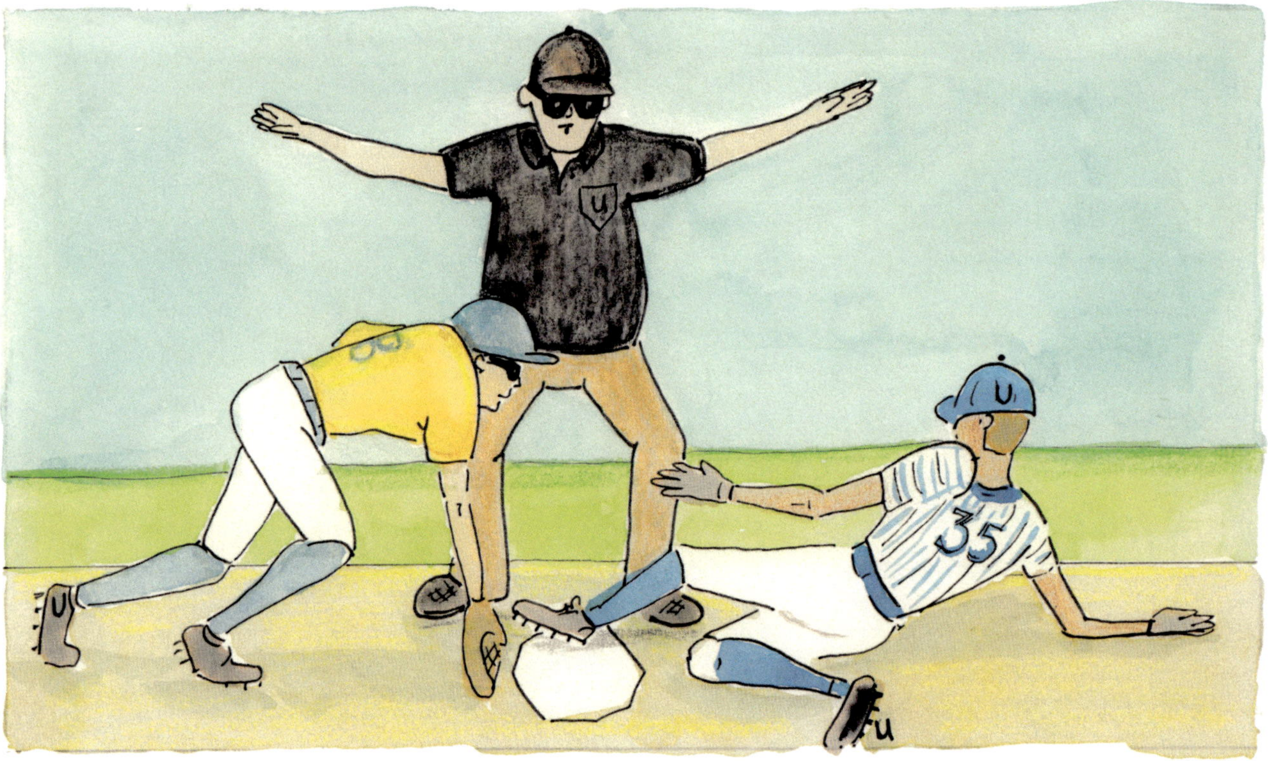
35

U is for the Umpire we see at a Blues game

V is for Valencia Peak,
which has its own acclaim

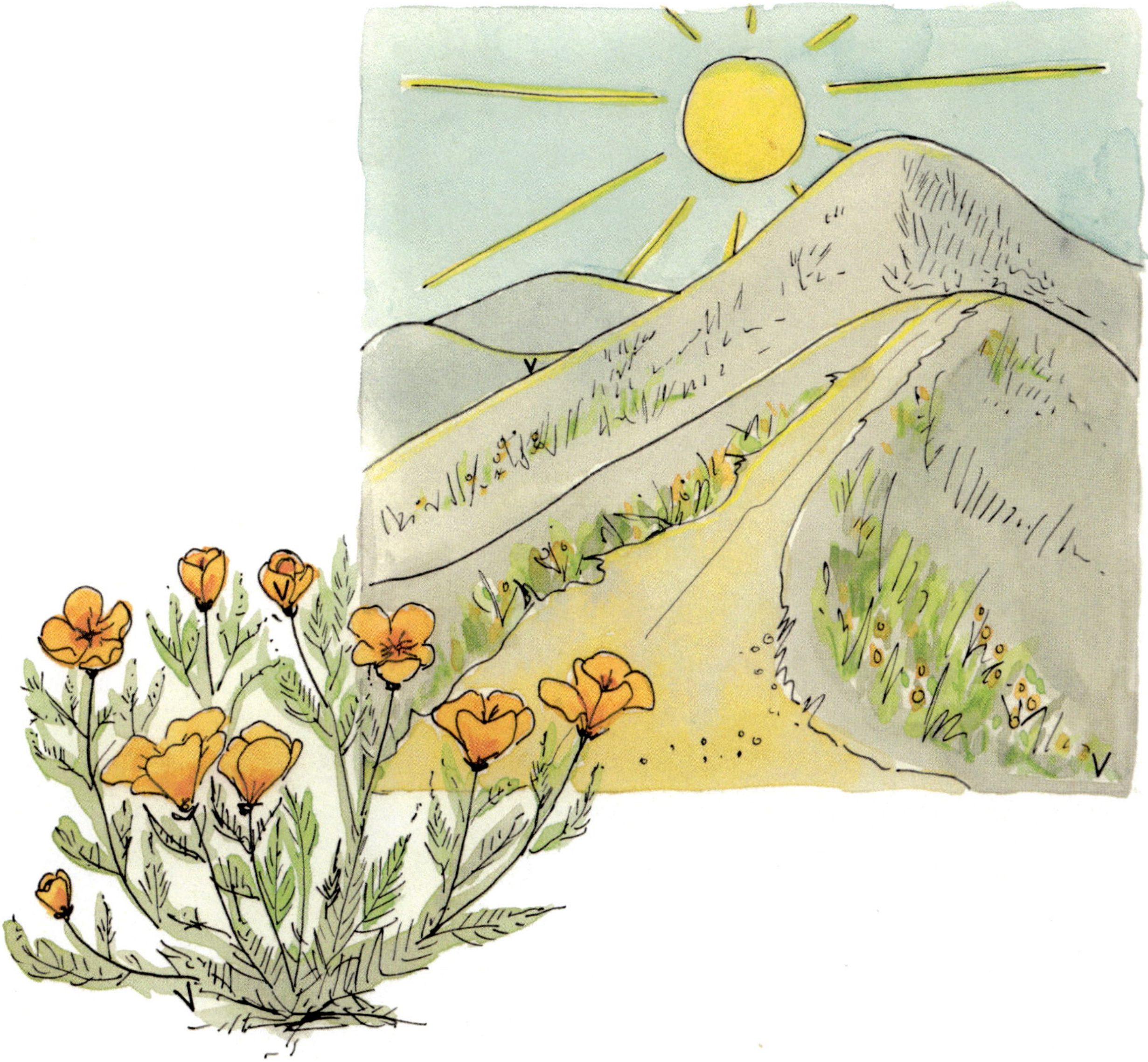

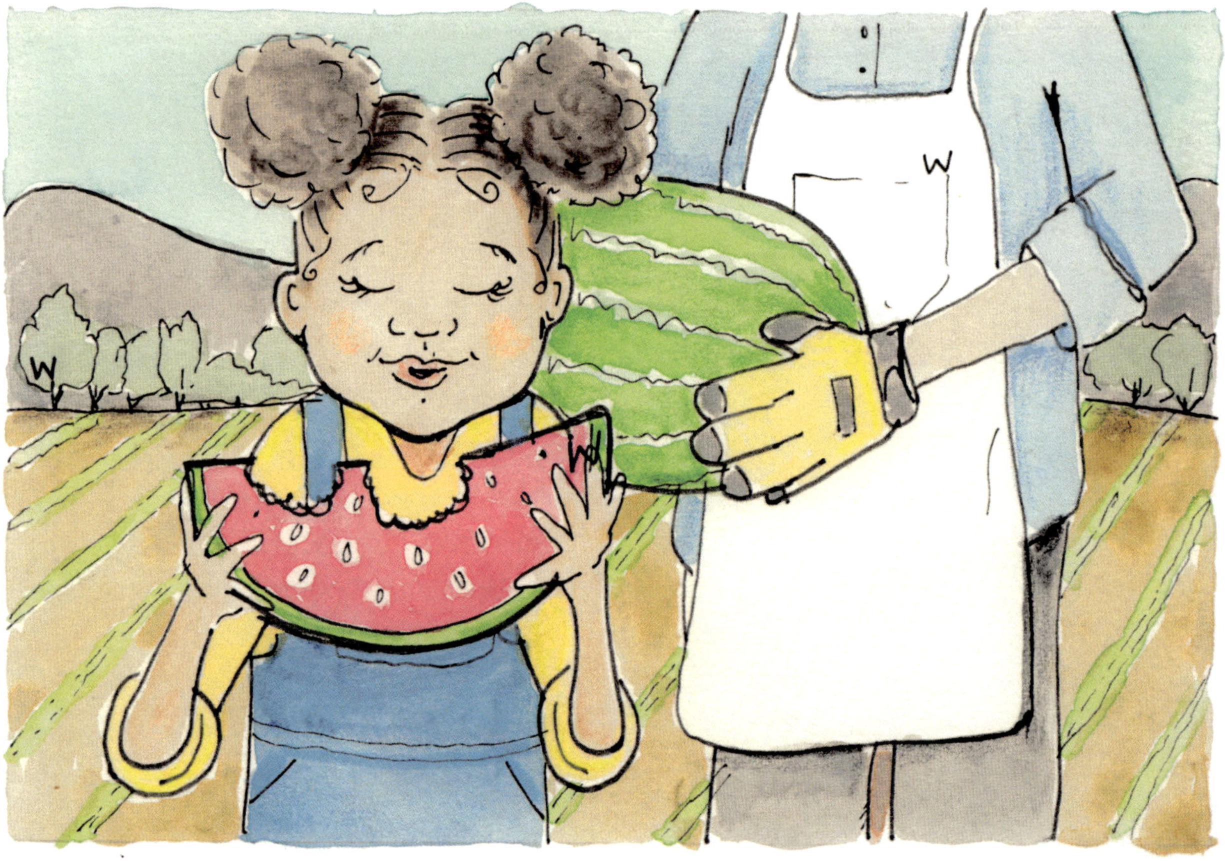

W is for the Watermelon that we like to eat from Talley

X is for the eXtra gross walk down Bubblegum Alley

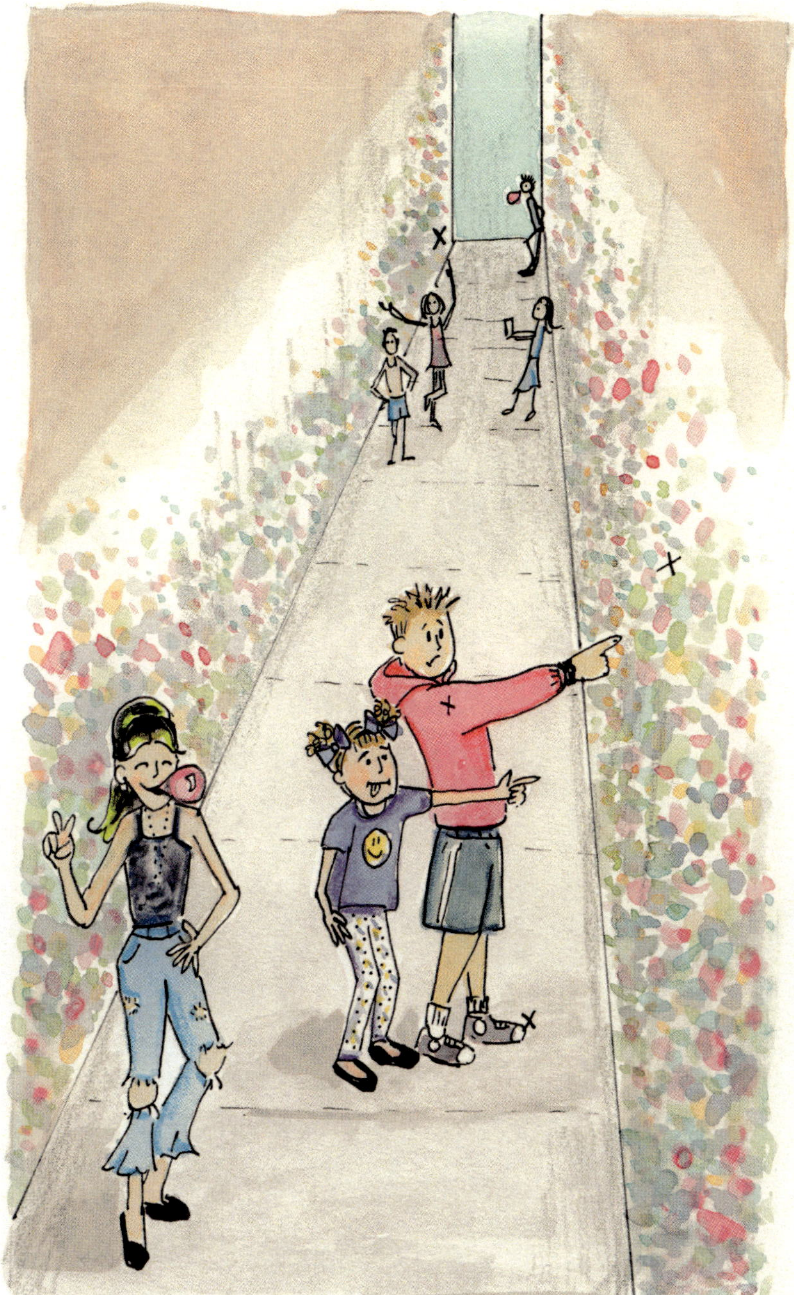

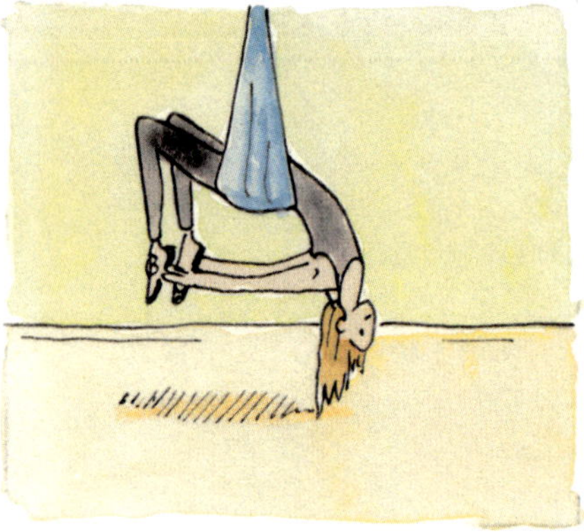
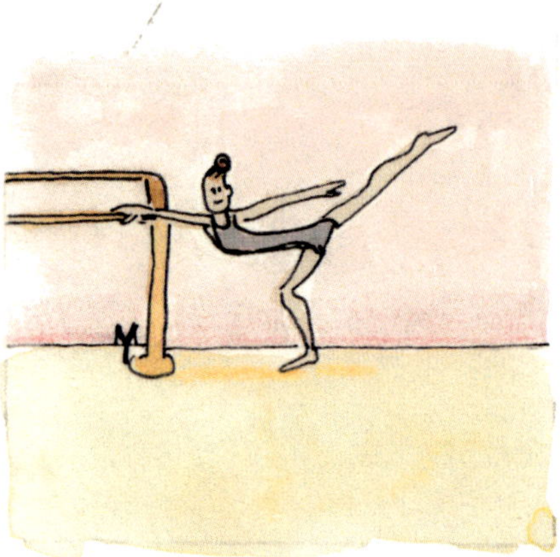
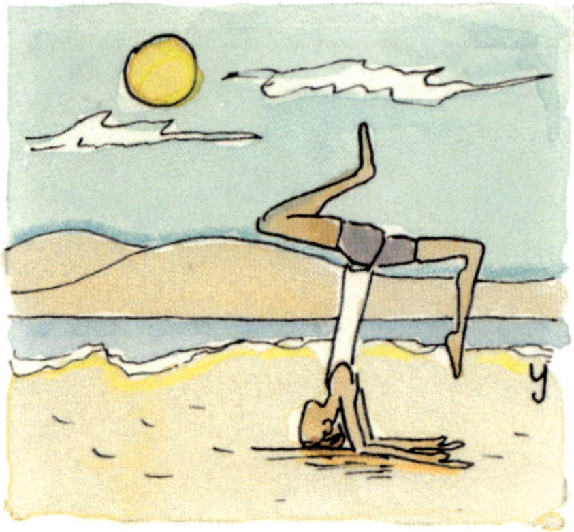
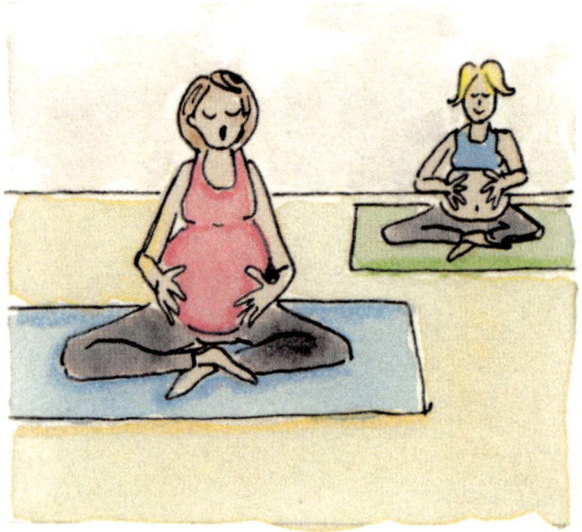
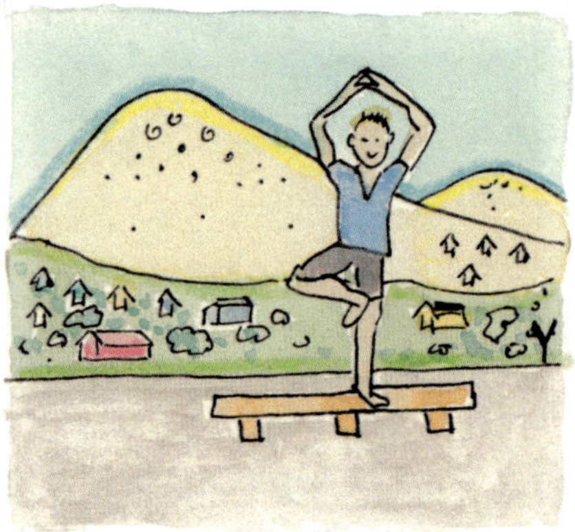
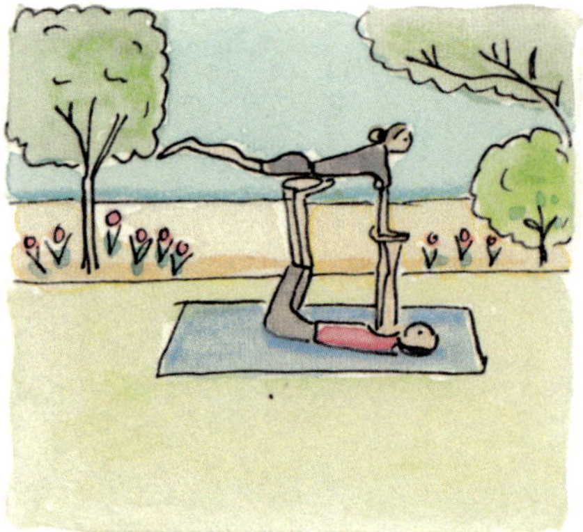

Y is for Yoga and
peoples' unique style

Z is for Ziplining which makes us smile

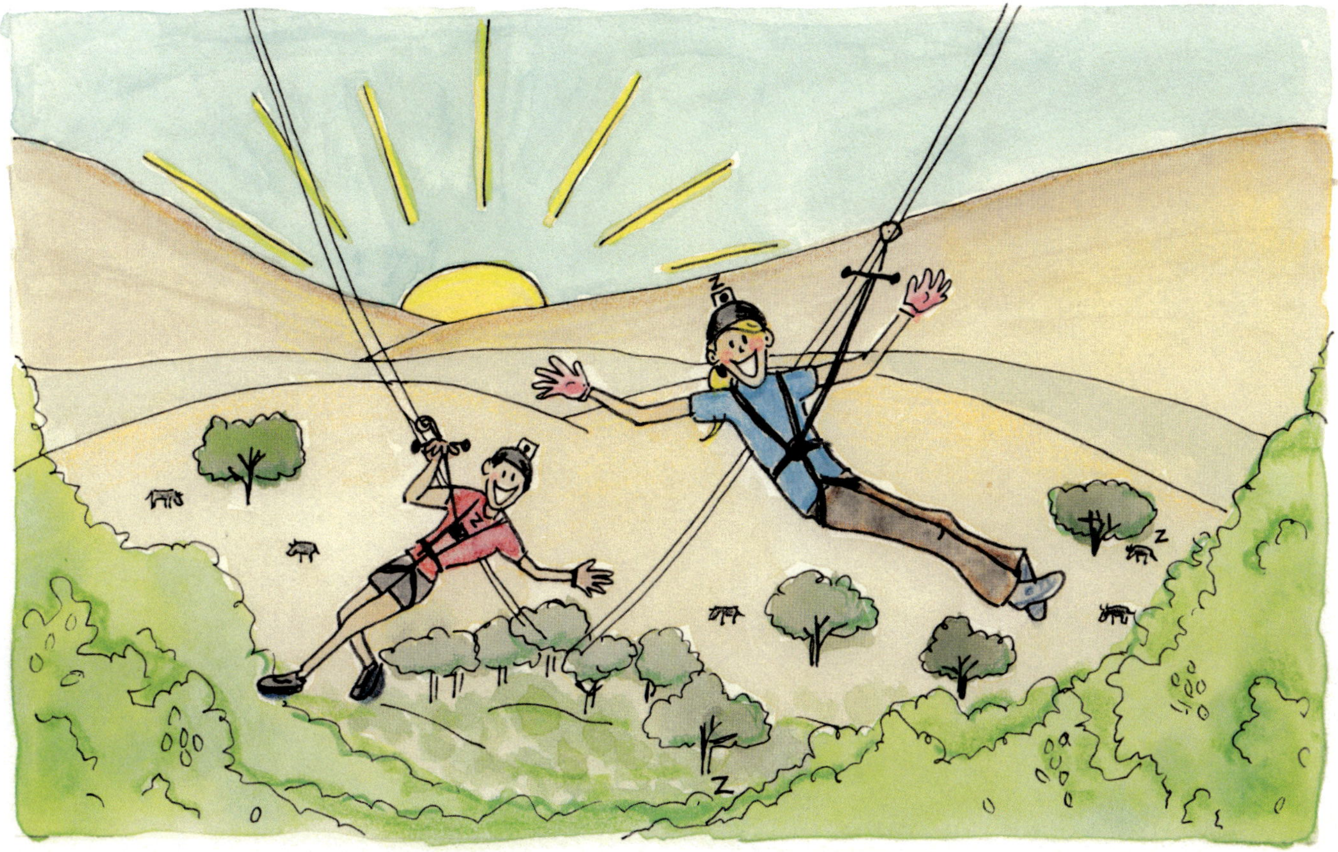

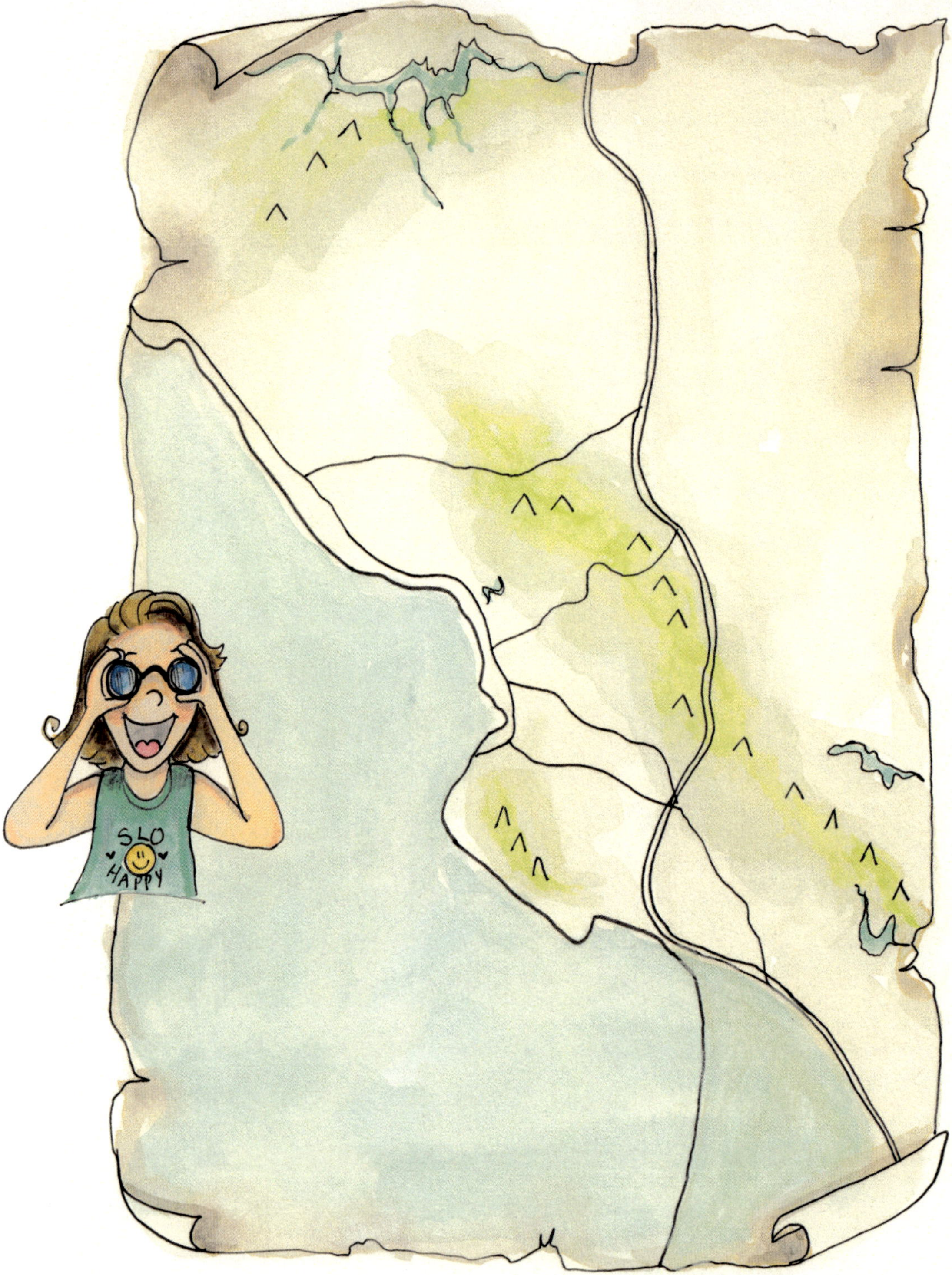
SLO
HAPPY

Exploration Challenges!

1. There are 2 uppercase and 2 lowercase letters hidden on each page. **Can you find them all?**

2. Pick a place in the book that you want to visit and **Go there!** Have fun adventuring!

- ☐ a: Gopher Glen
- ☐ b: beaches
- ☐ c: Brown Butter Cookie Co.
- ☐ d: Dinosaur Caves Park
- ☐ e: Elephant Seals
- ☐ f: Fiscalini Ranch
- ☐ g: Grover Beach thrift Shops
- ☐ h: Hearst Castle
- ☐ i: Negranti Creamery
- ☐ j: Jack Creek Farms
- ☐ k: kayaking
- ☐ l: Laguna Lake
- ☐ m: Monarch Butterfly Grove
- ☐ n: DANA Adobe
- ☐ o: The Great American Melodrama
- ☐ p: Pismo Beach
- ☐ q: Oceano Dunes
- ☐ r: SLO Railroad Museum
- ☐ s: Sunset Drive-In
- ☐ t: Montaña de Oro
- ☐ u: Blues Baseball game
- ☐ v: Valencia Peak
- ☐ w: Talley Farms box
- ☐ x: Bubblegum Alley
- ☐ y: yoga
- ☐ z: Margarita Adventures

Made in the USA
Middletown, DE
09 April 2024